Two Pianos, Four Hands—EARLY ADVANCED
Two Copies Included

BLUES CONCERTO

by EUGÉNIE R. ROCHEROLLE

Piano I

AF700052

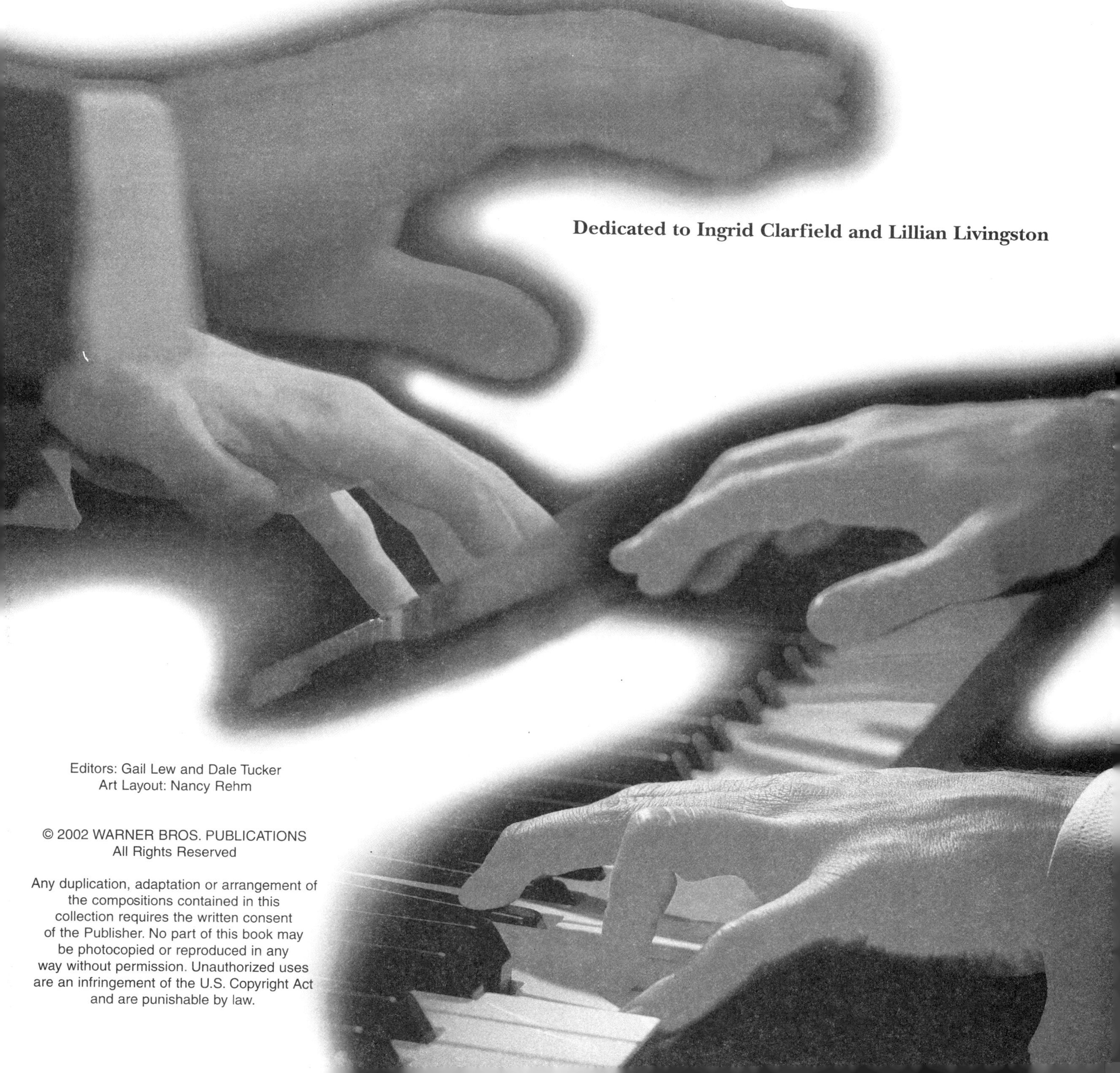

Dedicated to Ingrid Clarfield and Lillian Livingston

Editors: Gail Lew and Dale Tucker
Art Layout: Nancy Rehm

Eugénie Rocherolle

Composer, lyricist, pianist, and teacher, Eugénie Rocherolle began an early publishing career in choral and band music. In 1978, with the success of her first piano solo collection, she soon established herself as one of the leading American composers of piano repertoire. Her music is widely distributed throughout the United States and abroad.

A native of New Orleans, she graduated from Newcomb College of Tulane University with a BA in music. Her junior year was spent in Paris where she had a class with the late Nadia Boulanger. She was honored as the 1995 outstanding Newcomb alumna.

A "Commissioned by Clavier" composer, she was also one of seven composer members of the National League of American Pen Women whose works were chosen to be presented in a concert at the Terrace Theater in the Kennedy Center. Awards from the Pen Women include a first place for both piano and choral in biennial national competitions.

Mrs. Rocherolle's creative output also includes unpublished works in solo voice, chorus, and orchestra; musical theater; and chamber music for a variety of mediums. She is a member of the American Society of Composers, Authors and Publishers (ASCAP); Connecticut Composers Inc.; and the National Federation of Music Clubs. Her biographical profile appears in the *International Who's Who in Music, Baker's Biographical Dictionary of 20th Century Classical Musicians, International Encyclopedia of Women Composers, Who's Who of American Women,* and *Who's Who in the East.*

Mrs. Rocherolle has released recordings of her piano music, *Spinning Gold* and *Romancing the Piano,* and her Christmas arrangements, *Tidings of Joy,* on an independent label, Aureus Recordings.

Mrs. Rocherolle maintains a private studio where she teaches piano and composition.

BLUES CONCERTO IN C

EUGÉNIE R. ROCHEROLLE

10
mf
senza pedal
10
I
II
13
13
16
16

19
I
19
II
22
I
22
mf
II
25
I
25
II

28
I
II
31
poco rit.
Meno mosso (♩ = 96)
34
mp
con pedal

37
I
II
poco rit.
a tempo
poco rit.
a tempo
40
Adagio (♩ = 72)
8va
rit.
p
Adagio (♩ = 72)
rit.
mp espressivo
43
(8va)
*
**

I
II
poco rit.
accel.
rit.
Piu moto (♩ = 76)

55
I
II
poco rit.
a tempo
mf
58
8va
rit.
mf a tempo
a tempo
61
(8va)
rit.
Allegro, ma non troppo (♩ = 132)
f
senza pedal
Allegro, ma non troppo (♩ = 132)
f

64
I
II
67
8va
simile
70

73
(♩ = 126)
I
II
rall.
mp
poco rit.
con pedal
76
a tempo
accel. e cresc.
79
poco rit.
f
a tempo
rit.

82
Cadenza
I
a tempo
mp
simile
cresc.
85
mf
88
cresc.
Piu moto (♩ = 132-144)
subito mp
91
mf
cresc.
94
simile
f

97
100
poco rit.
8va
rit.
104
Allegro moderato (♩ = 152)
senza pedal
104
Allegro moderato (♩ = 152)
107
8va
107

110
I
110
II
113
I
113
II
116
I
116
II

119
I
decresc.
rit.
119
II
decresc.
rit.
122
Meno mosso (♩ = 92)
molto rit.
Adagio (♩ = 76)
mp
espress.
con pedal
122
Meno mosso (♩ = 92)
mf
molto rit.
Adagio (♩ = 76)
125
I
125
II

128
I
II
mf
poco a poco accel.
molto cresc.
131
8va
15ma
rit.
a tempo
l.h.
134
ff a tempo
f a tempo

137
I
II
Allegro (♩ = 144)
140
l.h.
r.h.
Meno mosso (♩ = 120)
subito mp
cresc.
poco a poco
143
poco rit.
Andante (♩ = 80)
f marcato

146
I
146
II
f marcato
poco accel.
poco accel.
149
I
rit.
8va
ff a tempo
accel.
149
II
rit.
ff a tempo
accel.
8vb
152
I
rit.
8va
152
II
rit.

(circa 6:30)

COMPOSER SPOTLIGHT SERIES

PIANO SOLOS

The *Composer Spotlight Series* introduces students and performers to the rich diversity of music composed by America's leading composers. Each volume will enhance the study of classical repertoire while providing students with music in a variety of motivational contemporary styles. The intermediate collections presented here will heighten the experience of practicing and performing for students of all ages.

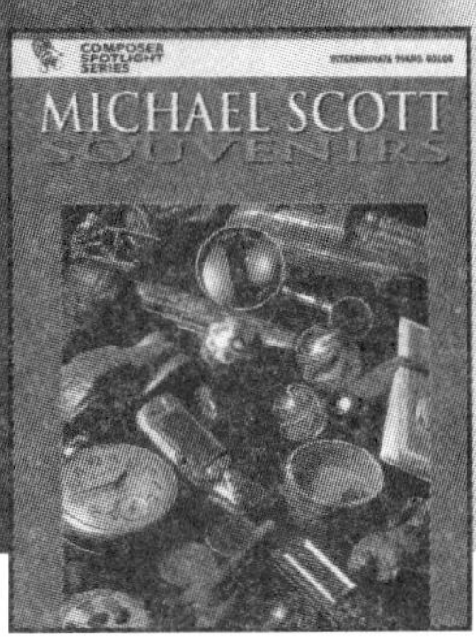

JOYCE GRILL

IN CHARACTER	(ELM00006) Intermediate
IN STYLE	(ELM02003) Early Intermediate
MOVIN' ON!	(ELM00005) Early Intermediate
RANDOM THOUGHTS	(ELM00007) Intermediate
REMEMBERING	(ELM00008) Intermediate
COUNTRY SCENES	(ELM02005) Elementary

BARBARA HARRY

SUMMER DAZE	(ELM01036) Late Elementary

BEATRICE A. MILLER

DAYTIME ADVENTURES	(ELM01038) Early Intermediate
NIGHT SONGS	(ELM01037) Late Intermediate

ELVINA PEARCE

ADVENTURES IN STYLE, Book 1	(ELM02006) Elementary
ADVENTURES IN STYLE, Book 2	(ELM02007) Late Elementary

EUGÉNIE ROCHEROLLE

FIVE SCENES	(ELM02004) Intermediate
KEYBOARD CAPERS	(ELM00024) Intermediate
KEYBOARD COLLAGE	(ELM00022) Intermediate
TOUCH OF BLUE	(ELM00023) Late Intermediate

ROBERT SCHULTZ

CHARACTER PIECES	(ELM00002) Late Intermediate
DAYDREAMS	(ELM00003) Late Elementary
IMAGES	(ELM00004) Early Intermediate
SCENES	(ELM00001) Intermediate

MICHAEL SCOTT

AUTUMN HARVEST	(ELM00015) Late Intermediate
CURIOS	(ELM00013) Late Intermediate
ENCORES	(ELM00014) Intermediate
SOUVENIRS	(ELM00016) Intermediate

AD0307B